The Wolf

Illustrated by Laura Bour
Created by Gallimard Jeunesse
and Laura Bour

MOONLIGHT PUBLISHING / FIRST DISCOVERY

Whose eyes
are these, gleaming
in the darkness?

The wolf's coat is thick and bristly.

Wolves run in single file, following in one another's tracks. There is only one set of prints, so it is difficult to tell how many wolves there are in the pack.

Its teeth are long and very sharp.

Incisors   Canines   Premolar   Molar

They are
the eyes of a wolf.

Sometimes all the wolves in a pack will start to howl. It's their way of warning another pack where they are.

People used to think wolves were dangerous, and
hunted them. Now there are only a few left in the wild:
in North America, Eastern Europe, and parts of Asia.

Wolves communicate...

Calm

Suspicious

On the alert

Wolves touch
noses to show
they are friendly.

using body signals.

Threatening

Giving in

Defeated

The leading male
and female are
the only couple
in the pack
to mate.

They rule the pack
and will use their teeth
to keep order, if necessary.

Each day the wolf brings food to his mate...

The she-wolf guards the entrance to her den. She growls
and snarls at intruders, and will attack any but her mate.

who cannot leave the den while her cubs are small.

There may be four or five cubs
in a litter. After they are about
one month old they begin
to play outside the den.

The mother takes the cubs to safety
at the slightest sign of danger. She carries
them gently by the scruff of the neck.

After sixty days the cubs
spend most of their time outside the den.

In the first warm days of spring
they spend their time playing and sleeping.

They fight and scrap.
The strongest cub will be leader.

Wolves are meat-eaters, or carnivores.

They enjoy chasing small mammals, like mice.

The wolf marks his territory with a few drops of urine. Then he scratches the ground with his back legs.

Wolves don't mind getting completely wet if they have to cross a river.

They also hunt bigger animals, like this hare.

Wolves curl up
in a tight ball to sleep.
They spend many hours
sleeping, especially
after a meal.

They need
a lot of water
to help them digest
the meat they eat.

This elk is old and sick. It has fallen behind
the herd, so the wolves begin to close in on it.

All the wolves in
the pack join in the hunt.
They chase the elk
until it is tired out.

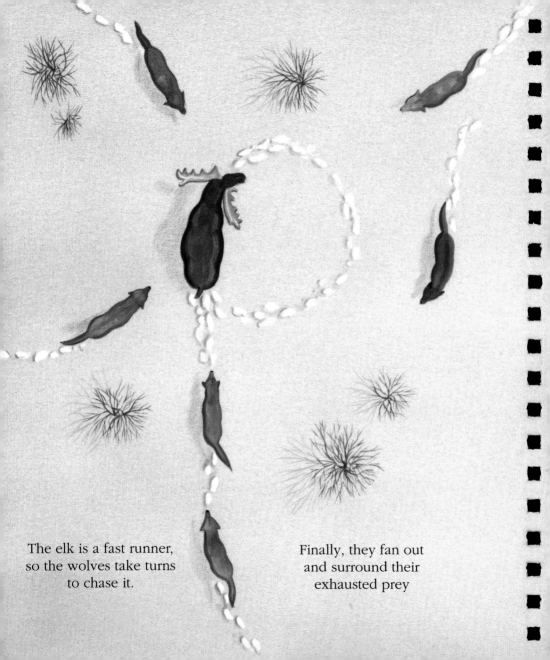

The elk is a fast runner,
so the wolves take turns
to chase it.

Finally, they fan out
and surround their
exhausted prey

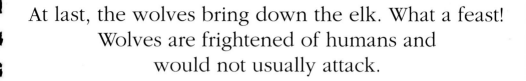

At last, the wolves bring down the elk. What a feast!
Wolves are frightened of humans and
would not usually attack.

A pack of hungry wolves
will strip a carcass bare,
leaving behind only
the elk's hooves and antlers.

There are few wolves left.
We must look after the forests
where they live.

In captivity, a caged wolf paces up and down.
He is bored and misses the wild.

Here are some close relatives of the wolf.

The tundra wolf varies in colour from white to black,
depending on where it is found. Wolves in the far north have paler coats.

Coyotes live in the deserts
of North America.

Foxes are smaller than wolves
and much more common.

Dingos are wild dogs.
They live in packs in Australia.

The Tasmanian wolf is extinct.
It was the largest meat-eating marsupial.
Like a kangaroo, it had a pouch for carrying its young.

You probably know the story of *Little Red Riding Hood* and the big, bad wolf.

Many fairy tales, legends and fables...

Romulus and Remus are said to have been brought up by wolves.

Aesop
wrote a famous story
about a wolf and a lamb.
Do you know it?

...tell stories about wolves.

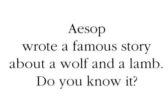

One fine morning,
Peter opened the garden
gate. Just at that moment the wolf
crept out of the forest...

This is the story of
Peter and the Wolf.
Serge Prokofiev
set it to music.

FIRST DISCOVERY: OVER 125 TITLES AVAILABLE IN 5 SERIES

AMERICAN INDIANS
ANIMAL CAMOUFLAGE
ANIMALS IN DANGER
BABIES
BEARS
THE BEAVER
THE BEE
BEING BORN
BIRDS
BOATS
THE BODY
THE BUILDING SITE
THE BUTTERFLY
THE CASTLE
CATHEDRALS
CATS
CHRISTMAS AND NEW YEAR
CLOTHES AND COSTUMES
COLOURS
COUNTING
THE CROCODILE
THE DESERT
DINOSAURS
DOGS
DUCKS
THE EAGLE
EARTH AND SKY
THE EARTH'S SURFACE
THE EGG
THE ELEPHANT
FARM ANIMALS
FINDING A MATE
FIREFIGHTING
FLOWERS
FLYING
FOOTBALL
THE FROG
FRUIT
GROWING UP
HALLOWEEN
THE HEDGEHOG
HOMES

THE HORSE
HOW THE BODY WORKS
THE INTERNET
THE JUNGLE
THE LADYBIRD
LIGHT
THE LION
MONKEYS AND APES
MOUNTAINS
THE MOUSE
MUSIC
ON WHEELS
THE OWL
PENGUINS
PICTURES
PIRATES
PREHISTORIC PEOPLE
PYRAMIDS
RABBITS
THE RIVERBANK
THE SEASHORE
SHAPES
SHOPS
SMALL ANIMALS IN THE HOME
SPORT
THE STORY OF BREAD
THE TELEPHONE
THE TIGER
TIME
TOWN
TRAINS
THE TREE
UNDER THE GROUND
UP AND DOWN
VEGETABLES
VOLCANOES
WATER
THE WEATHER
WHALES
THE WIND
THE WOLF

FIRST DISCOVERY / ATLAS
ANIMAL ATLAS
ATLAS OF ANIMALS IN DANGER
ATLAS OF CIVILIZATIONS
ATLAS OF COUNTRIES
ATLAS OF THE EARTH
ATLAS OF FRANCE
ATLAS OF ISLANDS
ATLAS OF PEOPLES
ATLAS OF SPACE
PLANT ATLAS

FIRST DISCOVERY / ART
ANIMALS
HENRI MATISSE
THE IMPRESSIONISTS
LANDSCAPES
THE LOUVRE
PABLO PICASSO
PAINTINGS
PAUL GAUGUIN
PORTRAITS
SCULPTURE
VINCENT VAN GOGH

FIRST DISCOVERY / TORCHLIGHT
LET'S LOOK AT ANIMALS BY NIGHT
LET'S LOOK AT ANIMALS UNDERGROUND
LET'S LOOK AT ARCHIMBOLDO'S PORTRAITS
LET'S LOOK AT CASTLES
LET'S LOOK AT CAVES
LET'S LOOK AT DINOSAURS
LET'S LOOK AT FAIRIES, WITCHES, GIANTS AND DRAGONS
LET'S LOOK AT FISH UNDERWATER
LET'S LOOK AT LIFE BELOW THE CITY
LET'S LOOK AT INSECTS
LET'S LOOK AT THE JUNGLE
LET'S LOOK AT THE SKY
LET'S LOOK AT THE ZOO BY NIGHT
LET'S LOOK FOR LOST TREASURE
LET'S LOOK INSIDE THE BODY
LET'S LOOK INSIDE PYRAMIDS
LET'S LOOK FOR LOST TREASURE

FIRST DISCOVERY CLOSE-UPS
LET'S LOOK AT THE GARDEN CLOSE UP
LET'S LOOK AT THE HEDGE CLOSE UP
LET'S LOOK AT THE OAK CLOSE UP
LET'S LOOK AT THE POND CLOSE UP
LET'S LOOK AT THE RAINFOREST CLOSE UP
LET'S LOOK AT THE SEASHORE CLOSE UP
LET'S LOOK AT THE STREAM CLOSE UP
LET'S LOOK AT THE VEGETABLE GARDEN CLOSE UP
LET'S LOOK UNDER THE STONE CLOSE UP

Translator: Simona Sideri   Editorial Advisor: Sarah Heath
ISBN 1 85103 239 8
© 1994 by Editions Gallimard Jeunesse
English text © 1996 by Moonlight Publishing Ltd
First published in the United Kingdom 1996
by Moonlight Publishing Limited, The King's Manor, East Hendred, Oxon. OX12 8JY
Printed in Italy by Editoriale Lloyd